THE VISION

"Something Seen
Through A Supernatural Event"

THE VISION

"Something Seen Through A Supernatural Event"

R. Vanderhoofven

THE REGENCY
PUBLISHERS

Copyright © 2022 by R.Vanderhoofven.

All rights reserved. No part of this book may be reproduced in any form or by any electronic or mechanical means, including information storage and retrieval systems, without permission in writing from the author and publisher, except by reviewers, who may quote brief passages in a review.

ISBN: 978-1-958517-62-8 (Paperback Edition)
ISBN: 978-1-958517-63-5 (Hardcover Edition)
ISBN: 978-1-958517-61-1 (E-book Edition)

Book Ordering Information

The Regency Publishers, US
521 5th Ave 17th floor NY, NY10175
Phone Number: (315)537-3088 ext 1007
Email: info@theregencypublishers.com
www.theregencypublishers.com

Printed in the United States of America

Contents

A Tribute xi

Preface xiii

Introduction xiii

Chapter 1 The Start... 1

Chapter 2 The Vision... 5

Chapter 3 It Speaks.. 11

Chapter 4 The Stroke... 17

Chapter 5 Cancer... 23

Chapter 6 Colonoscopy... 29

Chapter 7 Three Closest Men............................... 35

    Cornelius Vanderhoofven............................... 35

    Leon Louis LaBlue... 39

    Franklin Lee Vanderhoofven........................... 43

    Recap.. 47

Acknowledgments... 49

Epilogue... 51

A Tribute

This book is dedicated to my aunt, Selma L. Vanderhoofven, who left this world on April 20, 1999. Without her, God only knows where I would be today.

Preface

"And he carried me away in the spirit to a great and high mountain, and showed me that great city, the holy Jerusalem, descending out of heaven from God" (King James Version Rev. 21:11).

The story being told in this passage seems to be happening sometime in the future because Satan has finished his 1,000 years in the Abyss, the great battle that he lost, and has been thrown into the lake of burning sulfur. Good riddance!

The next thing to happen was the Great White Throne Judgment, where your name was found in the Book of Life, or eternal damnation done by each person is found in the other books.

(This is only an outline to show how we got here, where we are, to the Holy City, the New Jerusalem. This passage reads from Revelation 20:7 to 21:7.)

Finally, we come to the new Jerusalem. "And I, John, saw the Holy City, new Jerusalem, coming down from God out of heaven, prepared as a bride adorned for her husband"

(Rev. 21:2).

You see, this new Jerusalem will be a gift from God to those who have their names written in the book of life.

The following passage from scripture is what I wanted you to see. "In my Father's house are many mansions: if it were not so, I would have told you. I go to prepare a place for you" (Jn. 14:2).

Each person who has his or her name with in the book of life has a room in one of Gods mansions with his very own door.

Introduction

As a little guy, I often wondered what was "behind the door." When I became a little older, I found out it was Jesus at the door, but still the door was closed. As I read the Bible, I found where Jesus said: "Behold, I stand at the door, and knock: if any man hear my voice, and open the door, I will come in to him, and will sup with him, and he with me" (Rev. 3:20).

So, there was part of it. At this point I was in my late twenties and by this time had read my whole Bible from Genesis to Revelation.

It was about then that this passage jumped out at me: "In my Father's house are many mansions; if it were not so, I would have told you. I go to prepare a place for you" (Jn. 14:2).

By this time, I had formed a pretty good description on what it looked like, but I forgot one important factor. I forgot that I was the one who changed.

My aunt taught me how to receive a vision.

I learned that she was 100 percent Cherokee Indian, that she had married my father's oldest brother, but more important, she had been a Christian for about seventy years.

She was born February 7, 1907, as Selma L. Rhodes. She was married to Horace T. Vanderhoofven on November 20, 1935. She had three children. She died on April 20, 1999, and her resting place is Chandler, Arizona.

Here is the story.

This is one part of the story of God and the devil as seen by one of God's simple followers.

Chapter 1

The Start

"Go into your bedroom, close the door, and face it with your eyes closed. Block out everything, and see yourself passing through the door into another part of the house." That was all Aunt Selma said.

So I tried it. I went into the bedroom, closed the door, and faced the door with my eyes closed. I blocked out everything and saw myself passing through the door into another part of the house and back again. I tried it a number of times.

Each time I began, my goal was to have a vision. I tried going outside while my body remained inside. I tried to mentally walk from the backyard to the front and into the street. I walked past about three or four houses, and then I returned, and then it happened.

It had been raining steadily for about five or six days. I was repeating the exercise one evening, having been up the street once, when the sky became unusually light. I made it back and completed my exercise. I do not remember why, but I pulled the curtain back to see outside. Oh, my word! The sky was unusually clear and filled with the light of a full moon. This was the first time a vision had happened for me.

In another instance, a person approached me out of the blue. I stared at it, expecting it to talk, but it just belched. That was the first living being whom I had anything to do with.

The next time it happened was in my bedroom. I would have many visions in this room. It started when I saw a baseball diamond. It was an odd shape, and a man gave me a bat that was somewhat oversized. I stood with my bat, and a pitch was perfectly thrown. I swung and hit the ball completely out of the park. Another ball was thrown exactly the same way, and I swung the bat, but nothing happened. I tried once again, and the same thing happened: nothing. I looked at the bat, and wouldn't you know it, it had a hole in it he same size as the ball, right in the sweet spot.

I tried this once in a ballpark where many people sat in the stands. A lottery ticket appeared in my hand. So I laid it on the step of the stands. I went around the curve. On the next set of steps I came to, someone gave the lottery ticket back to me. I looked at it, but it was blank.

Another time, I remember coming upon a sort of Disneyland caricature that was about three feet tall. It stood beside a rock that was about seven feet high and eight feet long. I asked if it knew Jesus. It said nothing but pulled out a little stick that was about two feet long and began whipping the rock. This kind of whatever it was moved somewhat like a crab, with legs on either side of its body. It could move to the right or to the left.

I saw a group of people on the other side of the street; they just stared. Standing at approximately 5' 8" to 5' 10' tall, they appeared to be from a motorcycle group, although there were no motorcycles present. It appeared that they stayed together in pairs.

Then, the day came when suddenly something even more amazing happened!

Chapter 2

The Vision

A. Before the story I must tell begins, I must make a couple of points. The first point is as follows: "And the devil that deceived them was cast into the lake of fire and brimstone, where the beast and the false prophet are, and shall be tormented day and night forever and ever" (Rev. 20:10). You see that the devil has reached his final end. His life span, in this dimension, is over, but his final fall is sometime in the future, instead of now.

The second point is this: "And I, John, saw that Holy City, new Jerusalem, coming down from God out of heaven, prepared as a bride adorned for her husband" (Rev. 21:2)

The Holy City will not be released until the devil has been cast into the lake of fire and brimstone. Then, sometime in the future, the Holy City, new Jerusalem, will come down from God.

It is my belief that the vision occurs in new Jerusalem sometime in the future. God set this time to show me, one of his lowest creatures, the highest dimension there is. Here is my story.

B. The light came on, and there was Jesus, but we did not make eye contact. He was standing at the door made of six boards with a large arch over it. From Jesus' and my side of the door, there appeared to be no way to secure it, and some kind of vine grew around the door without a single leaf blocking it. I looked back at Jesus. He was still looking at the door when he said, "Follow me."

Immediately, I was standing in an open door with nobody around. I looked down the trail, which was a golden color, with each side a sparkling green. I looked again at the trail; it appeared to be about eighteen to twenty inches in width. I reached down to grasp a handful of what I thought was soil and brought it up to my eyes. It was powdered gold, which I released immediately.

I looked to my left. Beyond about four feet of grass, a stream ran parallel to the trail. It was about five feet wide and five inches deep and was filled with what appeared to be water. Suddenly, I was there, standing in the middle of the stream. I looked closer and was puzzled. It didn't really act like water. I took some of it in my hand and was amazed. It wasn't water! I held crystal that flowed like water.

There was one other thing: When I emptied my hand, it was dry.

I looked about twenty-five yards ahead between the trail and the stream, and saw what appeared to be a bookstand. A bookstand! What in the world was that doing there? Instantly, I was there. The bookstand measured about twenty-four inches high, twenty-eight inches wide, and sixteen inches deep. There was a book on the stand. The left side of the book was dark, and the right side was bright. Looking closer, I saw a sentence on the left side near the top, one near the middle, and one near the bottom. What was this book saying? Oh, hold it just a minute. All the righteous acts are recorded, and the unrighteous acts have been blotted out. So that is what it meant!

I turned around and saw a magnificent tree about fifteen feet away with a base approximately four feet wide. I looked, and I was there. But wait—I knew what this was. This was the Tree of life that bears twelve different kinds of fruit every month.

I faced the bookstand and tried to sit down, when, for just a second, I was weightless. I brought forth another thought: I was a spirit.

I began to wonder about what I could see across the stream. It looked like bare countryside, except for a mound about 100 yards away. I wondered whether there were a beautiful mountain scene over there somewhere. Suddenly, a rock appeared in my hand that measured about seven inches wide, four inches high, and a half-inch tall. I looked a little closer and there was a beautiful mountain scene on the rock.

Without thinking about it, I pitched it toward the countryside, and suddenly the mountain scene appeared, just as I had imagined it.

What might take seventy-five to 150 million years to move was moved in an instant. That's probably why Jesus said, "Because of your unbelief: for verily I say unto you, if ye have a faith as a grain of mustard see, ye shall say unto this mountain, removed hence to yonder place; and it shall remove; and nothing shall be impossible unto you" (Matthew 17:20).

I looked about 100 yards across the stream, and I was instantly there.

Looking straight ahead, I saw where the mound started. The base was approximately fifty yards and the top was about twenty-five to thirty feet in height. There was suddenly a tremendous sound; it was extraordinarily beautiful music. I looked around and picked up a single blade of grass. The sound was coming from the blade and all of the other blades, which numbered in the millions or possibly billions.

But wait—the grass didn't have a mouth. How could something sing without a mouth? I looked closer and realized that these millions, if not billions, of blades of grass sang using telepathy.

I gazed once more at he closeness of the mountains. They looked to be about ten or fifteen miles away but appeared crystal clear. How could this be? Not even the mountains should appear to be so close. But look here. I saw that there was nothing at all from here to the mountain, not even a single air molecule. That explained why I had a crystal-clear view. I then became aware of something: I did not need air to breath.

Now I had another question: Where was the sun? I looked where a normal person would look—to the sky. The sun wasn't there, but it had to be somewhere. Everything was lit up. I began to look around and—hold on just a bit—I had it. God was there, and the glory of God lit up virtually everything.

I looked at the mountains and suddenly I was there. Looking back, I saw that everything radiated a beautiful, sparkling essence. So, this was it—every time I thought about a place, I was there, no matter the distance. Take, for instance, the farthest known object in our dimension of reality, which is about 13.3 billion light years away. But with the Holy Spirit, I could immediately be there. I thought about a place down by the stream about thirty yards past the bookstand, and I was there. The golden path marked its end at the book stand. The stream made a forty-five-degree turn to the right.

When I looked in the other direction, it appeared as though the steam and ground ended about thirty yards from there. Further on, it appeared that the ground was about 1,000 feet below me. A city was located on the ground, but I could see no one there.

Now, here is a thought that I had been playing with: Where was the "mansion" that I had been hearing about? I then realized that "mansion" is a term that refers to something within our dimension of reality, and this was another reality altogether. In our dimension, we have to sleep somewhere, and shower somewhere, and generally take care of our bodies. But the next dimension doesn't require these things. So now it made sense to me. No place was needed to sleep or shower or generally take care of the other things in this dimension. So "mansion" doesn't refer to an indoor place; it refers to a place outside—and what an outside I had found.

Chapter 3

It Speaks

In the summer of 1999, I was driving a truck pulling a fifty-three-foot refrigerator van across forty-eight states. I was having a wonderful time with the Spirit as I drove.

One time I was travelling through Ohio, listening to a collection of gospel messages. That morning, I noticed that I had not listened to one of my favorite broadcasters for some time, so I turned on the radio and tuned into his channel. I listened for about fifteen minutes, and suddenly heard the Spirit when he said: "Get into prayer."

Suddenly, my mind changed, and I began receiving about three different frequencies all at once. Now, the radio did not change, but the telepathy that came was just about to drive me crazy.

I took the first off-ramp that offered a truck stop and started to pray. I prayed for about twenty to thirty minutes, until the mental messages finally stopped. That would be the last time I turned the radio on and looked for a broadcast by person who did not believe in Jesus Christ.

Then there was the time when I was in Pennsylvania at night and stopped to get something to eat. I found a place to park and began to walk into the restaurant. A man of about thirty-five to forty years old stood near the back door. He wore a jacket that was too short to cover his navel. His belly was too big. He was dirty, and he needed to shave. I made my way to the door in a kind of roundabout way. I had a nice dinner and headed back to the truck. I noticed that the man was not there anymore. I reached the truck and climbed aboard to pray, but nothing happened.

"But Spirit, where are you?" I asked, but still nothing happened. I tried for about fifteen minutes, and then I drove away.

About two days later it struck me. That man was meant for me. Oh, no. I had something that was meant for me to give to him: five dollars so he could get a shower. So What was I to do now? I knew; I made a promise that whenever I saw someone in need, I would be there to take care of that need. Each time I stopped some where, I looked and looked searching both the front door and the back. I did it when I got somewhere and when I left. Then, one day it happened.

I was shaving one morning at a Missouri truck stop, and a young kid (twenty to twenty- four year old) showed up looking for money for a shower. I told him to wait outside. When I finished, I met him outside and gave him the money. I asked if he had eaten breakfast, and he said that he had not. So, after he had taken a shower, he met me in the restaurant, and we had breathfast He was a Christian, which I learned as we talked.

When I was in Arizona about two months later, I found another fellow. He was having some kind of trouble with his car. I had a duty to him, so I asked about his car. His need was quite legitimate, so I helped him out.

One time, I was driving about forty or fifty miles northeast of Pierre (pronounced "pier"), South Dakota (which held the Capitol building). I passed them by forty or fifty miles and arrived around midnight, got out of my truck, and walked around for a while. The truck had a light green, twenty-four inch water pipe. The site was about a hundred yards off the highway, where the pipe was well below the ground. This was a pipeline, probably to carry water to Pierre. I got back into the truck and lay down to get some sleep. Suddenly, before any sleep had come, my eyes opened abruptly. It seemed that somebody had come, but I couldn't hear a sound. Still, I sensed there was someone there. I listened more carefully, but there wasn't anyone or anything present, as far as I could tell.

Not long after that, the Spirit's communication with me changed in such a way that it left me astounded. I met with my pastor and shared my experience. He seemed a bit disturbed because he developed a frown. He said that it seemed like something was not right, but he could not put his finger on it. My visitor came about two more times, and one day, the pastor suddenly said: "I know who it is now: It is the devil."

That hit me, in the spirit realm, like a Mac truck.

After much of my attention, this is what I found.

The Holy Spirit's voice is not a voice at all; that is, I don't hear him with my ears or inner ears but with my inner mind. The Holy Spirit's thoughts and my thoughts are one and the same; therefore, there isn't a voice to make out. When you hear him, you have to ask, "Was that him or me?" The last thing I want to cover here is the Alpha and Omega. God is present in everything from the smallest particles to the largest universes; from beginning to end. He is Alpha and Omega.

I hear the devil with my inner ear (telepathy). The devil's thoughts and yours are separate, which means the devil's voice is always discernible. The next step is knowing that the devils voice is higher, somewhat like a female voice. (Remember that we are dealing with a different dimension that does not have a male or female, where him and all of his horrid of demons are cast down to our dimension.) The best way to describe him is as one who operates totally in our dimension. He is completely obedient to time, and there is not a bit of truth within him.

I decided that the next time it came, I would demand that it leave.

I waited about two months, and the voice came back. It asked, "Do you want me as your father?"

I said, "No, get out of here."

It sounded like the same kind of female voice when it began, "But I never said—"

At this point, I turned the voice off. This was the same voice that had tempted Jesus.

In my case, I called it "the lying devil."

I have not heard this voice in my life since, but the devil's actions are another story.

Chapter 4

The Stroke

In late 2008, I found myself working for the same trucking company that I had worked for about seven years earlier. I say "worked," but I didn't work full-time. I would work four months with about two months off, then about three months on and two and a half off. You get the point.

When I began driving my pickup truck, I could usually find a parking spot with the other vehicles. Then I would find my truck in the yard, fire it up, and look for my trailer. Once I found it, I backed up to it. When the latch had found its mark, I got out and walked back to confirm that it had indeed found its mark. Then I would wind up the trailer's landing gear, and thump the sixteen wheels (the two front tires would not need to be thumped because I could visually confirm whether they were flat or inflated). Then I would roll up to the diesel pump and fuel up the tanks (one on each side) and the tank on the trailer because the refrigeration unit for the trailer also took diesel. I'd seen the refrigeration unit hold the trailer at twenty degrees when the temperature outside reached one hundred degrees.

On October 22, 2008, I had to make a delivery in Ithaca, New York. I pulled into the front parking area and shut my truck down. I looked at my watch, which read about 10:30 p.m. I got out of the vehicle, walked to the area where the merchandise would be unloaded, and made a mental note to myself: "Yep, this will do."

I figured this would get me to Rochester, NY, for a Kodak film load tomorrow afternoon. Little did I know that this was to be my home for the next seven weeks.

I climbed into the cab's sleeper for a good night's rest.

When I woke, it was 6:20 a.m. But wait a minute, my hand was paralysed. I started to get up out of bed and fell down. I thought, "My gosh what is happening? I scooted to the gear shift and tried to get up, with no luck. "Well, what do I do now?" I wondered. It was about then that someone knocked on the door. I could not answer, neither could I answer the second time someone knocked. I did not know why, but I couldn't. Someone knocked a third time, and after a short bit of time, two gentlemen opened both doors. I said, "Take me to the hospital," in my own mind, but it came out as gibberish. I do remember the time on my watch was 8:20 a.m. When both fellows climbed in and took hold of me, I felt safe. Then I passed out.

I woke on two separate occasions. The first was in the van; it lasted about five seconds. The second also lasted about five seconds.

Ithaca has a population of about 30,000 people. It is in the middle of the state measuring east to west and on the southern shore of Lake Cayuga. The distance to New York City is approximately 220 miles. Cornell University joins Ithaca on the east. Its enrolment is about 21,000. Cayuga Medical Center is about a mile on the left side of Lake Cayuga, and one of its specialties is the treatment of strokes. This happened to be the kind of condition with which I had been stricken.

I do not remember anything about coming out of the treatment center, which happened about a week later, but I remember

The Vision

my sons being there and a lady who asked for my insurance card. I told her I didn't know about it. I truly didn't. She would repeat it every morning (except weekends), but I still did not know. She asked every morning for about a week and a half, and then she quit. Looking back, she must have figured out that I was a veteran.

During the first week, I was there with my sons, who had come to see me.

I was delighted to see them. My first, Kihl, came by himself. His birthday is May 15, 1977. He did a tour in the Marine Corps from early 1996 to 2000. He was married at the time with a son.

My second son, Brody, was born July 13, 1979. He was a wrestler in high school and placed fourth in the South Dakota state tournament in his senior year. He was in the army from 2006 and has done one tour of duty in Iraq. He was single at the time.

My third son, Daniel, was born February 14, 1981 (Valentine's Day), and he brought his girlfriend with him. They left on the second or third day. Brody left on the fourth or fifth day, and Kihl stayed about a full week before he left.

I piddled around in the recreation room, and near the end, I took rides in a wheelchair and once toured out front.

After about six weeks in the medical center they told me, "All right, you are ready to go now. The only thing is you have to get somebody to give you a ride."

"Great! Here I am, about 2,600 miles from home, and I have to get a ride," I thought. So I dialed my number two son to see if he was busy.

Brody was stationed at Fort Hood, Texas, with approximately 41,000 other soldiers. Brody found himself in the First Army Division (with about 10,000 to 15,000 soldiers); however, only a few were scheduled to go to Iraq. Killeen is midway between

Dallas and San Antonio (about 150 miles from Dallas). It joins Fort Hood on the north side, and its population is about 125,000.

When Brody said he was coming, I knew we had time because one month was plenty of time to travel from Killeen, Texas, to Ithaca, New York, then from Ithaca to Livermore, California and then from Livermore back to Killeen. The head office told him to go ahead, so off he went. He arrived on Tuesday, December 9, 2008. Boy! That sure lifted my spirit, and after a short time, we left. Goodbye, Ithaca.

It was so good to be back on the road. We chatted about many things as we drove. One topic was his enlistment in the Army. He had finished one tour of duty in Iraq and had one remaining tour. Another topic was our hunting together someday.

We made it to Daniel's home in Livermore, California, during the early morning hours of Friday, December 12, 2008. It was quite a trip. We shook hands, and Brody left one day later.

My next task involved seeking a place in the VA hospital south of Livermore. It took five weeks, but I made it. I had one roomate, and we shared a doctor with many other men. The meals were satisfactory and came from an off-site location. One time, after lunch, a man came to give a talk. He had about fifteen patients, so I stayed to listen. He spoke about fly fishing and tying on fishing hooks and had a number of them for whoever wanted to attempt to tie one. My right arm was paralyzed, so I left after a short bit of time.

A young physical therapist was in the main building on the fifth floor. We started in the physical training room, then moved to the hallway. The hall started with sixty feet of corridor, took a left turn, went another hundred feet, and then turned back. But it didn't stop there. I started back to the hospital (the main building of the hospital was a little less than a quarter of a mile away) to where the hall formed a square with hallways that were each about one hundred feet long. I walked these hallways two times, or for approximately 800 feet, before I left.

Back in the main building, we began to ascend and descend a normal flight of stairs. We climbed up and down about twice.

The work day was also a visitation day. I grew up in Livermore, California, so visitation was not a problem. Ray and Bruce came with me. Allen came next. Then Jay came, and a couple of ladies wrote letters. Boy, I wasn't hurting for company.

One day, I went on the bus over the bay to Palo Alto. They wanted a computerized tomography (CT) scan so I got on the gurney and entered the machine. They took scan after scan. Slowly, I got colder and colder until I could not take any more, and informed them of such. I waited about five minutes, and they agreed that they had enough scans. I went back to a room, and a nurse gave me a warm blanket. Boy, that warm blanket covered me up for about fifteen minutes until I warmed up. I hoped they got what they wanted.

A young woman was in charge of our social activities; she scheduled some fun activities. We also had some really nice mini-buses at our disposal. I took two or three bus rides.

Well, three months was about up. I want to go to the hospital again someday when I am well again.

Chapter 5

Cancer

During September 2010, I had a large number of white blood cells, about fifteen times what would seem normal, during a regular blood test.

Living in Nampa, Idaho, with a VA center about twenty miles away, I prepared for the second test, known as a biopsy.

For the biopsy, the doctor used a rather large needle, and it surely didn't feel comfortable. They took a number of tiny cylinders, which were a little smaller than a pencil lead, from the material to be tested. I found it painful to sit on the bus home, but I made it.

The hospital called me the next day. I had tested positive for cancer in the prostate gland. The VA has been fairly forthright in regard to Agent Orange, which was used quite liberally throughout South Vietnam to clear the jungle in which enemy soldiers hid. It is a disease-causing agent, and if people come in contact with it, sometime in the future they will pay. One of the first things I did was file for Social Security under the Agent Orange Act.

I found Physician Assistant Rod Riggs at the VA center. His office was located in the spetcialty clinic. We sat down in his office, and he began by saying that they would be sending me to Seattle,

Washington, as it had the closest raditation machine, which was near Nampa. I thought about that for a moment, and then said, "If they want to send me to Seattle, perhaps they could send me to the San Francisco Bay area to Palo Alto instead. I have three boys who live about thirty miles from there." He thought a moment and said, "Wait a minute here," and started to write.

I waited about five minutes, and then I asked what he was writing about.

He said he was fifty-seven years old and that if I did not get this, then nobody should. I guess he was referring to the stroke that I had suffered. After approximately ten minutes, he finished writing; then he submitted the document. Next morning, the phone rang. I answered, and it was PA Rod Riggs.

He said, "You got it."

He meant that I would stay here and go to a civilian radiation machine in Boise. Hooray, I thought, but little did I know what would happen next.

I went to the west side of Boise in the middle of December for a preliminary appointment.

I met Stephanie, the receptionist. She answered the phone, made appointments for patients, and generally took care of all the things that the radiation therapist did not consider necessary. She let someone know that I was there and, before long, another person came from the back room. Her name was Kelly, and she was a radiation therapist. We wasted little time and started down the hall. At the bend were two monitors on a shelf with two desks built against the wall. (I will cover these a little later.) We turned left and, after another walk entered another room. Once we arrived, it turned into a double room that led to a very narrow room with a table built for two on one side and monitors on each of the computers. We were introduced to another radiation therapist,

The Vision

named Anna. Once we entered the door, we took a quick right turn through a second door. The two rooms were separated by a glass wall from the door to the other end. The second room housed the CT scanner. This machine weighs in at approximately 30,000 pounds, and the voltage is rated in the thousands.

I got onto the bed, and Kelly made everything very comfortable. She took some small BBs and glued them onto my skin where the cancer was present. She then went into the other room where the switch on the computer activated the CT scanner. It put forth a quiet kind of hum.

Kelly told me that when she starts in the morning, one of the first things she does is start the CT scanner because it takes about twenty-five minutes to warm up. When she is ready, she puts her finger on a switch that delivers a CT image.

She sat down and put the computer to work. It communicated with the CT scanner to deliver imaging of various areas, including the pelvis. The project was completed in less than three minutes.

I went through the series of scans and didn't feel a thing.

At this point, Kelly turned the CT scanner to idle mode, reentered the room, and replaced the BBs with spots of permanent ink. All done; the radiation therapist helped me up and accompanied me back to the waiting room. Before long, I was introduced to Dr. John E. Gamboa, who provided a quick rundown of his building and what it housed. We scheduled Monday appointments to cover any problems that might occur. Then, a nurse came in and said that she had the telephone number for the VA Minibus Program and that she had reserved seats for me from December 20, 2010, until approximately the end of February 2011. All looked well for next Monday, so we shook hands, and I departed. I also discovered that day that the doctor was a Christian.

As planned, I came in the next Monday as planned and found that everything was ready to go. This time Anna led me straight to the back of the building; we made a 180 degree right turn around a three-foot-thick wall, and there it was, the linear accelerator that delivers sufficient speed to the intensity modulated radiation therapy equipment.

I laid down on a bed. Anna put my cane against the counter and fashioned a pillow for my head and a wedge for my legs. She then tied my toes together to prevent movement. I was to hold onto a blue ring with both hands; this was done to prevent movement and confirm that the bed was level. At this point, Anna went into the hallway.

There were two monitors in the hallway. The first one was monitoring me to make sure I did not move. The second one kept track so that the appropriate level of radiation was not exceeded.

All of this was because of cancer and how it is, for most people, curable. It all began with the discovery of a tumor. A large percentage of cancer is discovered by tumor. Being in such a large group, it is only natural that most people choose radiation, the most effective form of treatment for treating malignant tumors. I opted for radiation treatment. It started with shooting an X-ray not just one but eight times. A circle is the best way to start, and eight positions comtpletes the circle ($8 \times 45° = 360°$). After forty-seven treatments, I can now say that I am cancer free.

When the treatment was done, the intensity- modulated radiation therapy machine was reset. Anna reappeared, removed the restrictive items, and returned my cane. We exited together.

The weeks began to wear on me, and when we had about three weeks left, it became easier to ask the driver to take me home at about 10:00 a.m. rather than back to the VA where I had to wait from 2:00 to 4:00 p.m. to go home.

The Vision

I finally made it to the end, but it seemed like the forty-seven treatments would never be over. Of my five symptoms, I will share this one with you: I turned white as a ghost.

The time came for Dr. Gamboa and me to part. My ordeal with prostate cancer had lasted about two months. We wished each other well and parted.

As for the cancer, the prostate-specific antigen (PSA), is a protein produced by cells of the prostate gland. A reading of .5 (nanograms of PSA per millilitre of blood) to 1.0, which is okay. In contrast, the test results that I had received before, of around 8.5, meant "Look out!" Four years have passed, and I am able to say I am still free of cancer.

Chapter 6

Colonoscopy

When I turned sixty-two, I decided to have a colonoscopy. It was my first one, and doctors recommend having them done every five years beginning at age fifty. I made my appointment and showed up on October 6, 2011.

When I showed up, the nurse said, "Oh, we usually give someone a gallon of Golytely and a motel room the night before the appointment, but I see you are operating with a stroke. Here, take this and we'll prepare a room."

The VA takes pretty good care of me, so I didn't worry about it.

They gave me a room and a gallon of Golytely to drink. They also gave me a nightgown to wear. About halfway through the drink, it started to work. Now I began to see why they gave me a gown and a portable toilet. I finished with the drink in about one-and-a-half hours and with the toilet about four hours after that. I watched TV for about one hour afterward and then fell asleep.

Morning arrived, and I got ready to go. After about one hour, a nurse came in and asked, "Are you ready?"

I reply, I said, "Ready!"

After a short walk we turned into an examination room, when another man entered to have his examination.

It wasn't long (about twenty minutes) before he was pushed out: he was unconscious. I was next. I underwent anaesthesia and passed out suddenly.

I was out for the duration of the examination, so I got Lessie Schoenfelder, the nurse, to fill me in on what happened.

The colonoscopy on October 7, 2011. The scope was approximately five feet long and 7/8 inch in diameter and had assorted lights and channels with which to work. I had a white LED bulb, a channel for a jet of water, a channel for a high-speed jet of water, and a channel for a number of different tools to pass through.

First, Dr. Matthew Sericati started putting the Olympus video colonoscope into my bowel. Then, he inflated the bowel with air. Once finished, it was time for the Olympus video colonoiscope to start the process of going through the descending colon, laterally through the transverse colon, then down the ascending colon. It was the ascending colon where the doctor found the trouble. Sericati used the hot snare cautery tool first. It was used on a polyp in a piecemeal fashion because a 1 3/8-inch polyp was too big to remove in one piece. Sericati also used two resolution clips to prevent bleeding and Carrlocke injection needle to inject some India ink to permeate the area so it could be readily identified. He then used a Roth Net to readily remove all polyp material. Finally, he used an Argon plasma cogulator to stop all oozing and bleeding. There were two small polyps in the ascending colon that were not removed due to a pending appointment. The air was evacuated, and the endoscope was withdrawn.

This was the first part of Schoenfelder's story. The second part starts momentarily. I'll start where I left off.

The next thing I knew, the bed was in the same place it always had been. The nurse said that larger polyp would more than likely bleed, but would likely not carry disease; however, although the two small polyps would likely carry no disease and would not bleed, it was far easier to deal with one than two.

It wasn't very long before I was back to my room, where I proceeded to put on my clothes. By that time I finished, the room nurse came in and said the doctor wanted to see me again in three months to "tie everything together." She also said I was free to go.

Time passed, and I was off to the hospital again. I did all the same things, and like before I was placed under anaesthesia.

Nurse Sohoenfelder filled me in on what happened again.

On January 18, 2012. Dr. Paul Baehr returned the endoscope to the ascending colon. Near the India ink he found a small bit of polypoid tissue, about 1/4 inch in length, that he used a hot snare to remove. He also located two small polypoid lesions and removed these with a cold snare. The air was evacuated, and the endoscope was withdrawn.

Like before, I got dressed, but this time I went out the emergency room exit. I waited a short time until Pastor Blankenship arrived in his SUV. We finished our trip by talking about a number of different things, and then we said goodbye and he left.

I said the following prayer before my appointment in January: "Lord, I now start my offering at 20 percent."

Approximately two days later, in the first week of January 2012, I saw something in my inner vision, and said, "A poem! Well, I guess I had better copy it down." Then I copied it down on the last page of the book of Revelation. After the sermon at church the next time, I took it to the pastor and asked him to read it. He read it and said, "Oh, I see you wrote it." He read it again and, "I will hang this somewhere on the wall."

R. Vanderhoofven

About three weeks after the pastor read the poem, he asked if I had seen it. I said no I had not. He pointed to the back room off the sanctuary. I went to the room and opened the door, and there it was, hanging on the wall. It's still there today.

Chapter 7

Three Closest Men

Cornelius Vanderhoofven

My grandfather, Cornelius Vanderhoofven, was born October 13, 1871, in Indiana. He was the oldest of four boys and three girls.

On August 20, 1905, he married Effie Ola Matheson of Scotch-Irish descent. He was seventeen years older than she was, and they had four boys and one girl: Horace, born in 1906; Harry, born in 1908; Harvey, born in 1914; Francis, born in 1921; and the youngest boy (my father), Franklin Lee Vanderhoofven, born April 26, 1923.

They settled on a dugout house for their first home in Oklahoma. My grandfather was a farmer most of his life, but preferred owning ducks. He also had a fondness for the constellations. He would get on the roof with Francis and Franklin and point out the constellations. More often than not, he would have to wake them up to get back down.

Once, when Cornelius was sixty-two and the youngest (dad) was ten, he said, "Let's go chop some cotton."

They didn't get too far before he said, "I'm too old, and you're too young. Lets go home."

One time, a bunch of gypsies wanted to paint the roof a reddish color. It didn't look too bad at first. Then, when it rained, it all washed out. Turned out it was motor oil and some reddish coloring.

In 1934, they moved to a rental house on Sunset Boulevard in Los Angeles, California. It was the first time that they ever had running water and electricity where they lived.

Aimee Semple McPherson, the founder of the International Church of the Foursquare Gospel, had preached for many years. She moved to LA in late 1918 and in December 1927 founded the church. Cornelius began attending McPherson church in 1936, when he was approximately sixty-five years old.

By 1944, Frank had enough money, due to his service injury, to bring Cornelius and his wife to Tulare, California to build his own house. That was the first time he owned his own home.

Cornelius figured that the most he ever made in one year was $50. Then, one day in 1945, he had a stroke that affected his speech. A few days later, he had another one that finished him off.

The date was June 29, 1945, in Tulare, California.

One thing that he always said was, "It's better to keep your mouth shut and be thought a fool, than to open it and remove all doubt."

Leon Louis LaBlue

Leon Louis LaBlue was born October 7, 1902, near Houston, Texas. He moved with his family to Johnson Mill Creek, Oklahoma. He was nineteen when he married Annie Flowers and started a family. Their firstborn was a boy named Jack LaBlue, who was born in 1921 at Johnson Mill Creek. The second child was Virgil LaBlue, who was born in 1923 in Chandler. The last child was Jernice LaBlue (mom), who was born on June 8, 1928 in Chicksha.

Time took its toll on Annie LaBlue, and it started with the loss of her hearing. Her hearing became so bad that she was committed to the mental hospital for being deaf. (During the 1930's a person who lost his or her hearing wondered, "Why doesn't anybody speak to me anymore?" The hearing person, however, saw a non- hearing person as a person whole mind has gone blank.)

In 1936, what was left of the family moved to California. It wasn't long before Leon bought a lumber yard to keep himself busy. An elderly man worked for him as a part-time employee. I was about five years old when we brought a load of lumber home. It took all night long; it was the crack of dawn before we made it home to Tulare, about 260 miles away.

Leon found a way to acquire homes with little money by finding which way the highway went and offering to move the house for no down payment. He would then disassemble the house (usually in two pieces) and place the pieces on wheels, which were then moved to a vacant lot. He then removed the wheels, put the house back together, placed it on the ground, hooked up the running water and the electricity, and collected the rent.

One year, when Jernice was listening to the Giants of San Francisco, California, she invited Leon LaBlue and his wife to visit one of the Houston Colt .45s games. As the game got going, we noticed that Juan Marichal was pitching for the Giants. As it continued, the game became one between Juan Marichal and the Houston Colt .45s. By the ninth inning, Juan had a no- hitter going against the other team.

Leon said, "It looked like the ball was going 100 miles per hour."

Brock Davis was the last batter for the Houston Colt .45s (now the Astros). He was the only Colt player on his team that had four at batts on that day and had a .222 batting average. Brock Davis waited for the last ball thrown by Juan Marichal. Juan wound up and threw the pitch, but Brock decided not to swing. Ed Bailey, the catcher, caught the ball, and Ed Sudol, the home plate umpire, called Brock Davis out. Juan had just pitched a no-hitter against the Houston Colt .45s. It was his only no-hitter.

Leon liked to fish, and one time around 1962, we went to a stream that was all dried up but variously sized ponds of water were left behind. We worked our way down, finding pools of different sizes, when we spotted a rather large one that was approximately forty feet across. We worked our way to it when, all of a sudden, a beautiful rainbow trout darted from our location to the other end. He didn't waste much time, and pretty soon "papa" (what the grand kids called him) had a treble hook on the line and began snagging for him. After about twenty minutes, he got him! We measured him at twenty inches.

One time, we decided to catch chipmunks. Papa made a three-foot square out of some two-by-fours, and then he put a wire screen on one side. He drilled a large hole on the outside and mounted a can. He then had a six-inch stick with a string tied to it. We found some food for the chipmunks in the mountains. We placed the two-by-fours under the screen wire; we propped up the trap with the stick and led the string about seventy-five feet away. It didn't take long to catch four chipmunks. I kept them for about a year until I found them dead one day; they had received too much sun.

When I was about fourteen, we headed up from Tulare to Firebaugh (in the South Central Valley) to meet the scale master. After weighing our truck, we headed out to one of the farms. They loaded our truck (our truck was good for 2.5 tons), and then we went back to the scale, where we found out we had just about 4,000 pounds of watermelon at 0.75 cents per pound, or $30. We made it to just past Burney in a day and a half. We then loaded about one day's worth of watermelon sales in Papa's pickup truck, which he stashed at his home. We headed northeast, going from town to town. In each town, we went to the general store. When a store bought the watermelon we sold, we moved to another town. When a general store refused to buy any watermelons, Papa sold watermelons at housed on the side of the road, and I sold on the right. Either way, we made money. At noon, we found a place for lunch, cut up a watermelon, and didn't get up until we were done. We would then find a fishing hole.

Leon was sixty-seven in 1970, and that year was full of bad news, starting with Leon being diagnosed with pancreatic cancer. Leon fought it at the Loma Linda Medical Center in California, but it was no good. He died at age sixty-eight on August 25, 1971.

Franklin Lee Vanderhoofven

Franklin Lee Vanderhoofven was born in Texhoma, Oklahoma, on April 26, 1923. Shortly thereafter, the family moved to Oakwood, Oklahoma.

When Franklin was eleven years old (1934), his family moved to a rental house on Sunset Boulevard in Los Angeles.

He never had money for marbles, and therefore used aluminium foil shaped like marbles instead. He was playing one day, and one of the "marbles" found its way into a light socket. That caused a fireball big enough to make Frank a believer.

Cornelius was one of Aimee Semple McPherson's followers at that time. One night, they all assembled for prayer, including Frank. They concluded the prayer, but Frank needed more time, so they continued. It was around that time when Frank slumped over, fast asleep. You can't imagine what Frank faced when he got home.

As Frank was in high school, he raised homing pigeons. He got in touch with somebody at the cemetery who needed some doves for burials. The homing pigeons working in place of the doves and, unlike the doves, could fly back. Frank said he bet he got the same homing pigeons back after every burial.

Then December 7, 1941, came around, and everything changed. December 7 was the day Japan bombed us at Pearl Harbor. It changed everything, and two days later, Frank joined the US Navy. He completed his training and then went shipboard. Frank was assigned to the *USS Helena CA-75*. On November, 12, 1942, Frank and another fellow went to the top of the smokestack because the Japanese were somewhere nearby. Suddenly, out of nowhere, a Japanese shell hit the *Helena*. Franks friend died and

Frank was wounded. As he woke in the early morning hours, he noticed that a small group of sailors had climbed up the smokestack. They handed Frank the ladder and headed for the sick bay. After being at the sick bay for a while, Frank learned that a piece of metal had gone through one of his legs, that another had gone through one of his shoulders, and that another had taken out his elbow, limiting his movement. Someone commented that it was Friday the 13th. That was the last of the war that Frank saw.

Two to three years passed, and Frank still didn't have a car. Whenever he needed to go somewhere he just hitched a ride. One early evening he got a ride to Tulare. He rode with a large family (six or seven children) to get something to drink. He said goodbye, and they parted. Down the road was a set of railroad tracks. Frank watched as the family approached the tracks, and just as the station wagon touched the tracks, killing the entire family. Frank wondered if everybody would have made it if he had stayed in the car. We would never know.

He met Jernice (my mom) in March 1948. They married six weeks later, on April 25. My birthday is on July 15, 1949; Terry was born in 1951 and Laurie (was adopted) was born in 1963.

In January 1957, he started the job that he would keep until he retired, as a researcher for the government at Lawrence Livermore National Laboratory.

He collected old bottles to pass the time. He would take a long rod (about six feet by one-quarter inch) to an old bar that used to have an outhouse and was just dismantle and probe the ground with the rod. When he found a place where the ground was soft, he knew that was where the outhouse had been; however after so many years it would be nothing but dirt and glass. He used to have a fellow dig with him sometimes, and they split the profit. A single-family home would have a couple of dozen bottles from which to choose, but the local bar had hundreds to pick through.

The Vision

Then the day came when he went for a colonoscopy. Everything seemed to be going well until the doctor looked in the colonoscope. He closed everything up and ordered immediate surgery. The day was Friday.

The surgery occurred a short three days later, on a Monday. The surgery went as planned and about eighteen inches (more or less) of the large intestine was removed due to diverticulitis. (When the colon produces pouches in the side wall, this condition is called diverticulitis.) The surgery went well, but for some reason, Frank was not responsive. They went back the next Friday morning and discovered a massive leak. They fixed the leak and gave him the strongest antibiotic available. That initially appeared to take care of the problem, but two days later, when the day nurse checked out, the night nurse checked in and found Frank's temperature spiking to 109 degrees.

The funeral took place on January 14, 2005, at the San Joaquin Valley National Cemetery in California.

Recap

I've told these stories about the three men to whom I was closest to state the following:

Cornelius Vanderhoofven had a stroke, and it killed him. My stroke did not kill me.

Leon LaBlue had cancer, and it killed him. My cancer did not kill me.

Frank Vanderhoofven had something growing in his lower bowels that killed him. I had something growing in my lower bowels, but it did not kill me.

Each one of these men had a disease, and it killed him. I had all three of these diseases and was cured.

The devil is a liar. He looks for whatever will make half-truths. Whenever he gets involved with someone, a disease, physical or mental, is certainly not far behind. Jesus best summed it up this way: "The thief comet not, but for to steal, and to kill, and to destroy: I am come that they might have life, and that they might have it more abundantly" (Jn. 10:10).

The End

Acknowledgments

Front Matter

Luke Joseph Duncan

Chapter 4
Kihl Vanderhoofven, *Brody Vanderhoofven, Daniel Vanderhoofven, Ray Alsdorf, Bruce Frame, Allen Ohren, Jay DeCaen

Chapter 5
PA Rod Riggs, Stephanie Harmison,
RT Kelly Davis, RT Anna Leatham, Dr. John E. Gamboa, Bob Prunty

Chapter 6
RN Lessie Schoenfelder, Dr. Matthew Sericati, Dr. Paul Baehr, Pastor Blankenship

Chapter 7
Terry Vanderhoofven, Laurie Vanderhoofven
Keola Walter, editor

*Brody is not the name of my second son, but has been used for the sake of privacy.

Epilogue

So many people dismiss any thoughts of the devil by relating him to a fairy tale, but this couldn't be further from the truth. To those who believe he is nothing but a fairy, he is quiet, and he stays hidden. Why shouldn't he? They all belong to him.

It all started with Adam, who took and ate some fruit from Eve, who had taken fruit from the forbidden tree. Adam transferred all of the earth to the devil. He and everyone on the face of the earth, both now and forever more, were forever condemned.

Then came Jesus, who accomplished the following: "Then Peter said unto them, repent, and be baptized every one of you in the name of Jesus Christ for the remission of sins, and ye shall receive the gift of the Holy Ghost" (Ac. 2:38).

So now we have the two sides. One side is hopelessly lost; no matter what they do, they are going to hell in the end. Alternatively, people can make Jesus Christ the Lord of their life with the indwelling of the Holy Spirit. How do people prove they have the indwelling of the Holy Spirit? They speak with other tongues.

You choose.

www.ingramcontent.com/pod-product-compliance
Lightning Source LLC
LaVergne TN
LVHW091048100526
838202LV00077B/3246